UP CLOSE

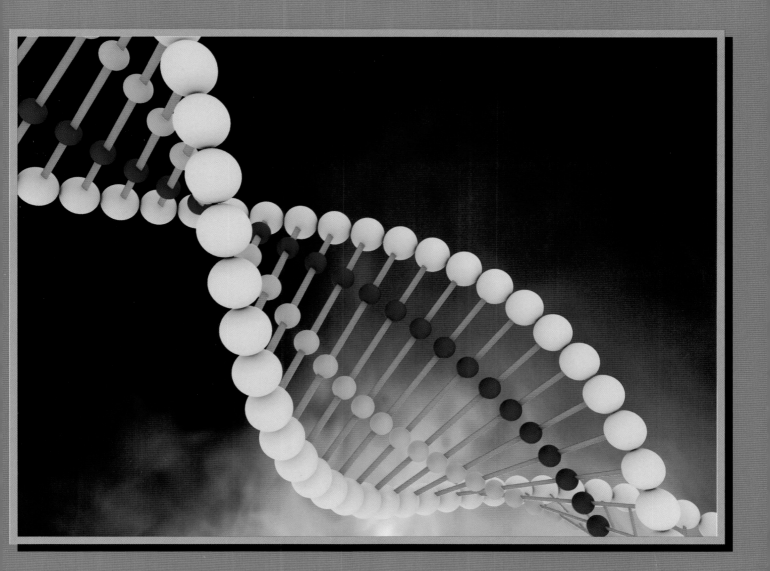

Human Body

PAUL HARRISON

W
FRANKLIN WATTS
LONDON • SYDNEY

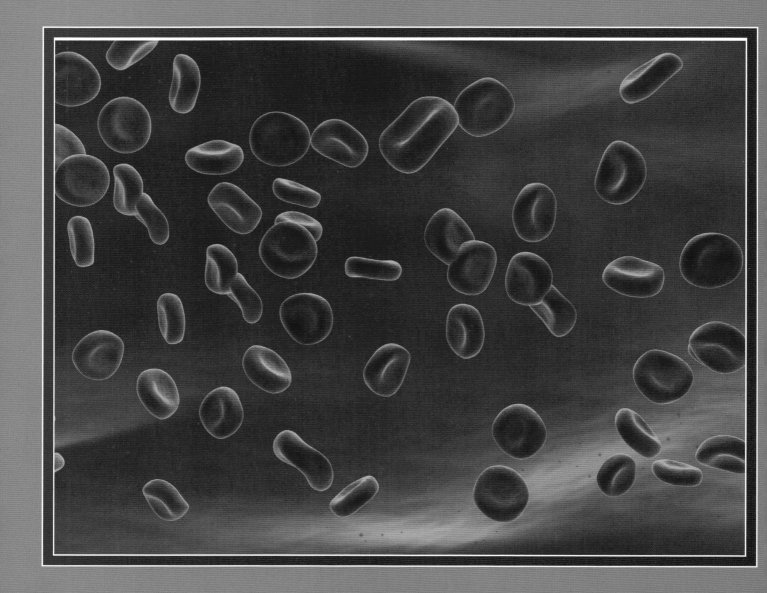

Published in 2009 by Franklin Watts

Copyright © 2009 Arcturus Publishing Limited

Franklin Watts
338 Euston Road
London NW1 3BH

Franklin Watts Australia
Level 17/207 Kent Street
Sydney, NSW 2000

Author: Paul Harrison
Editor (new edition): Fiona Tulloch
Designers (new edition): Trevor Cook, Sally Henry

Picture credits: Corbis: 4 top and bottom, 17 top, 20 bottom; Getty: 6 bottom, 9 top and bottom, 21 bottom; Rex: 5 bottom, 12 bottom; Shutterstock: title page, 2, 5; Science Picture Library: 6 right, 7 top, 10 top, 11 bottom, 13 top and bottom, 18, 19 top and bottom, 20 top, 21 top.

A CIP catalogue record for this book is available from the British Library

Dewey number: 612

ISBN: 978-0-7496-9211-7
SL000956EN

Printed in China

Franklin Watts is a division of Hachette Children's Books, an Hachette UK Company
www.hachette.co.uk

Contents

What a Wonderful Body

Skin, hair, blood, *muscles*, organs, *veins* and *arteries* — all in one neat package. You'll be really surprised what wonderful things are going on inside the human body.

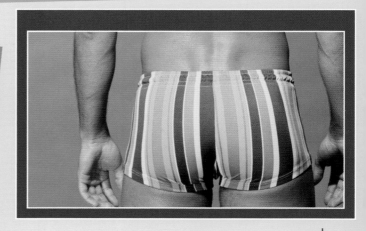

BIG AND SMALL

The biggest muscle in your body is the gluteus maximus – that's your bottom! The smallest bone in the body is the stirrup bone inside the ear – it's only 2 millimetres long.

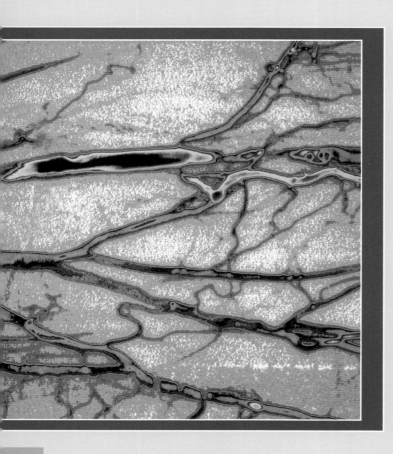

TUBES

Our bodies are full of tubes, or veins and arteries, which carry blood round the body. Including the tiniest, called *capillaries*, there are 100,000 kilometers of these tubes in the body. That's enough to go round the moon nine times!

STRETCHY

The body is amazingly flexible. Think of a pregnant woman and how her womb has to get bigger to accommodate her growing baby. Her body has to be really stretchy!

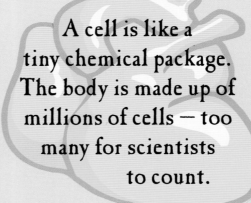

A cell is like a tiny chemical package. The body is made up of millions of cells — too many for scientists to count.

TOP-HEAVY TOTS

Our large brains make our bodies quite unstable. That's why toddlers fall down so often.

Super Structure

Our bones hold us up and make us look like humans, but that's not the only job they do. The skeleton is a really super structure.

MISSING BONES?

There are 206 bones in the human body. Surprisingly, babies have over 300. This is because babies' bones are quite soft and many of them fuse and grow together.

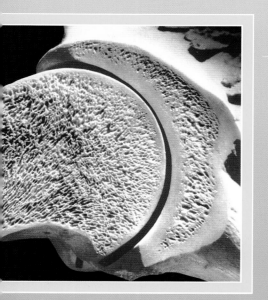

HARD SPONGE

Bones are strong, but not solid. Inside, they are like a honeycomb – filled with tiny holes. Outside, they are smooth and hard.

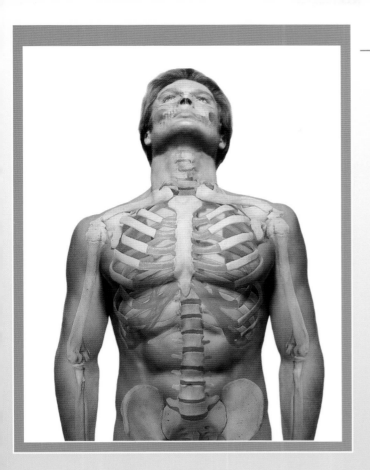

MULTI-TASKING

The way bones are arranged, they protect as well as support your body. The ribs curve round to shield the lungs and heart and the skull protects your brain.

Some young bones are made from *cartilage* — the same stuff that a shark's skeleton is made from.

GROWING

As we grow, so our bones get bigger. In fact they keep getting bigger until our late teens. Growing never stops. Bone needs to renew itself as old bits dissolve and new bits replace them.

BARE BONES

Inside the bones is a substance called marrow. This produces blood cells – you'll find out more about what they do on page 21.

When children are little, their bones are renewing themselves every two years!

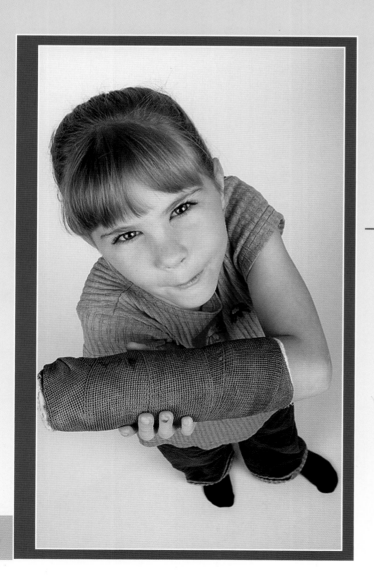

BROKEN BONES

A broken bone will take about 12 weeks to heal. It only gains the full strength of mature bone after around 18 months. In adults, it can take up to two years.

On the Inside

S ome of the most important parts of the body are your *organs*. They each do a specific job. Here are some of the major ones.

HEART OF THE MATTER

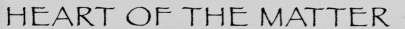

The heart is a muscle that moves blood around the body. Blood flows into the heart through the veins, passing through four chambers inside it before exiting through arteries. Heartbeat – around 70 times a minute – is the sound of blood being pumped from one chamber to another.

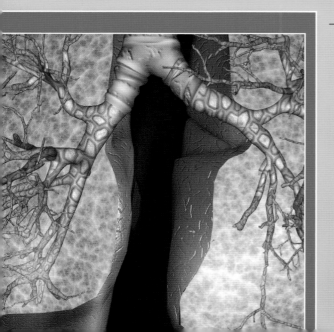

DEEP BREATH

The lungs contain little bag-like sacs which fill with air when we breathe in. Capillaries containing blood surround each sac. The blood absorbs oxygen from the air to take round the body.

KIDNEYS

The kidneys are the two organs that remove waste and excess water from your blood. The liquid product (urine) is sent to the bladder where it's stored until you go to the toilet. The kidneys also control the amount of certain chemicals in the blood.

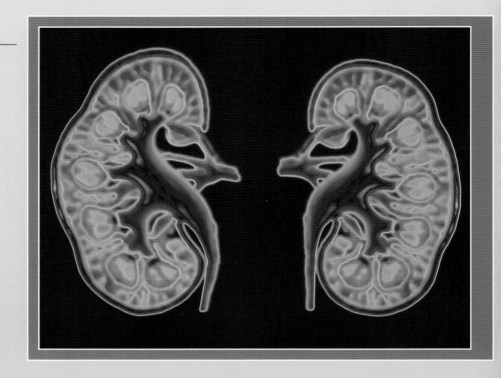

Some scientists think the appendix helped our ancestors digest tough food — we just don't need it any more!

BODY CHEMISTRY

Your body's biggest organ is the liver. It makes chemicals the body needs from the *nutrients* in the food we eat. It also produces the substance that makes blood clot if there is an injury to the body, like a cut.

MOUTH PARTS

The body starts digesting food in the mouth. Glands in the mouth produce saliva (spit) which begins to break down certain foods. Saliva is also necessary to help us swallow food. It's why our mouths water at the thought of food when we're hungry.

THE STOMACH FOR IT

The collection of organs that deal with food is called the digestive tract. When you eat something, it goes first from the mouth to the stomach, where you start to digest, or break down, your food. It is then pushed through the long, tubular intestine, where further stages of digestion take place. Waste is passed out at the end.

On the Outside

Bones, blood vessels, organs: we need something to hold everything together. It keeps your insides in — it's skin!

STRETCHY ORGAN

Your skin is your biggest organ and does really important jobs. It keeps out germs and harmful *ultraviolet* rays from the sun. It provides a layer of insulation, helping to keep the body at an even temperature.

STRAIGHT OR CURLY?

Our hair comes out of little holes in the skin called follicles. The shape of the follicle decides what kind of hair you have. A curly shaped follicle results in curly hair, a straight one means straight hair.

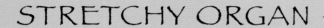

BUMPS

When it's cold, we get goosebumps because our skin contracts, pushing the hair up off the skin. Furry animals do this and it increases the amount of air trapped in their fur, improving insulation.

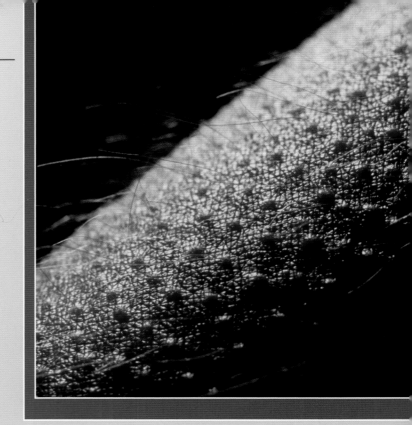

Your skin is constantly dying and re-growing — a lot of the dust around you is actually dead skin!

LAYER UPON LAYER

Skin is made of three separate layers. First, the outer, protective layer is the epidermis. Next, the middle layer, the dermis, is where hair follicles and sweat glands are. The bottom layer is the hypodermis. It attaches the skin to the rest of the body.

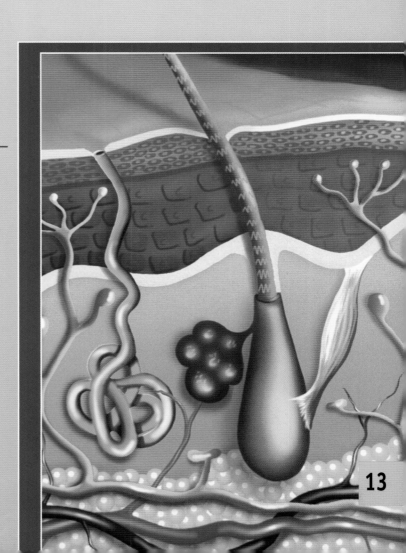

13

HAIR FORCE ONE

We have two kinds of skin on our bodies, the kind that has hair growing on it, and the sort that is found on our hands and feet without hair, called glabrous skin. Hairy skin varies from the kind on your scalp with hair you have to cut, to the kind on your arms with hairs that never get longer than a few millimetres.

The average adult has 2 square metres of skin which weighs about 3.2 kilograms.

UNIQUE FEATURES

The underside of our feet and hands have ridged patterns on them called friction ridges. The purpose seems to be to aid gripping. But we probably associate them more with identifying people. No two fingerprints are alike – even those of twins.

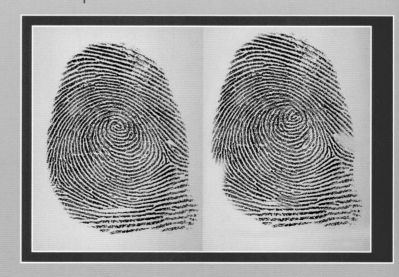

14

Sense and Sensation

Our senses give us awareness of what's around us. Without them we couldn't really do anything at all. Having senses really does makes sense!

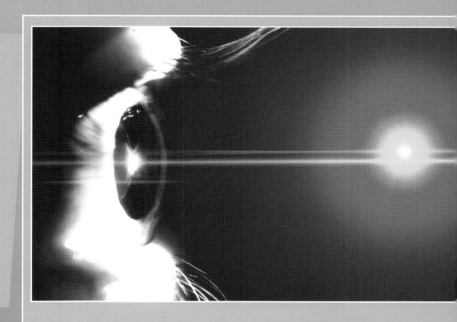

TOUCHY FEELY

The nerve endings send messages to the brain when we touch something. Touch receptors are grouped where they are most useful, such as the fingertips and the tongue.

EYE EYE

When we look at something, the light from it enters the eye, is flipped over by the lens and falls on the retina – the screen at the back of your eye. A signal from the *receptors* in the retina goes along the optic nerve to the brain, which flips the image the right way up again.

IMAGE CONSCIOUS

Your eyes can tell you what colour and how far away something is. But staring at one thing for too long can strain the eyes. So don't watch too much telly – those eyes need protecting!

Most people recognise five senses — hearing, sight, smell, taste and touch. Scientists also count the ability to feel heat, cold, pain, and balance.

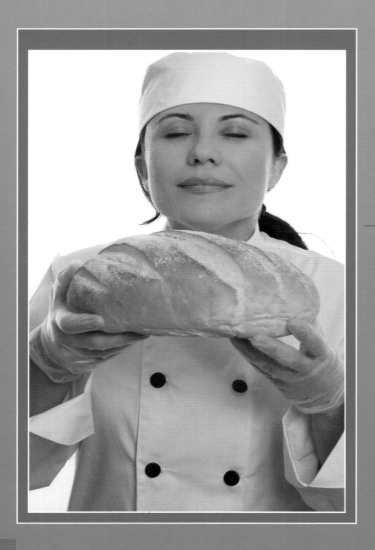

STINKY

Your sense of taste depends very much on your sense of taste. Your nose is more discerning than your tongue and can pick out hundreds of different smells. In fact, food doesn't taste the same if you have a blocked nose.

TASTY

Your tongue is covered in tiny taste receptors. They can only distinguish between five different tastes – bitter, sweet, sour, salt and umami. This last one is a particular taste that comes with many foods, including meat and cheese.

WORK SENSE

People with highly developed senses of taste and smell work in the food and perfume industries. Expert tea tasters use their taste buds to ensure consistent quality. Perfumers use their noses to test fragrances for new perfumes. So look after your senses – you may find one day your work depends on them!

Brain Box

There are machines that can do the work of most of the organs in your body, at least for a short time, except one — the brain.

USE IT AND GROW IT

Different jobs are done by different parts of the brain. The left side is the creative side. The right side deals with logic and calculation. If you use a particular part of the brain a lot, it tends to get bigger.

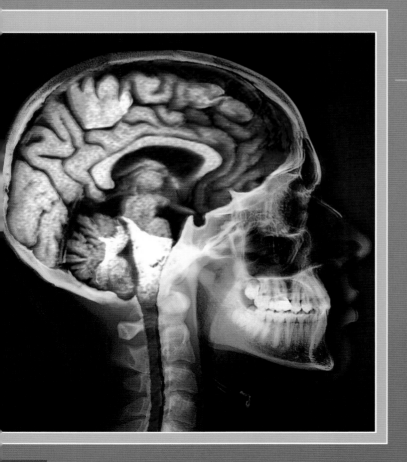

WHAT IT DOES

Your brain is your body's own supercomputer. It processes all the information from your senses, controls your breathing and stores your memories. While it does all this, 24 hours a day, it allows you to think about something else entirely or just go to sleep!

GLOWING

Scientists don't know exactly how the brain works, but they can see brain activity using special scanners. The scanners show which bits are active by lighting up the areas being used. This helps our understanding of how the brain works.

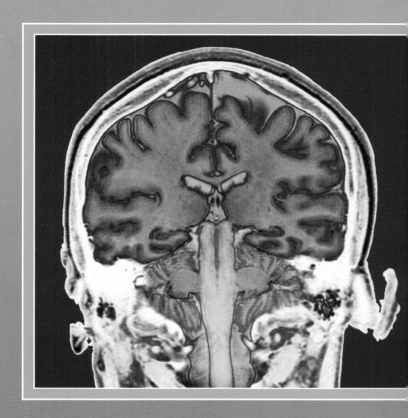

WHAT IT LOOKS LIKE

The brain looks a bit like a squidgy peach stone. The cerebrum is the largest part. It is split into two halves called hemispheres. Below is the cerebellum, and coming out from the bottom is the brain stem. The whole thing is surrounded by a thin *membrane*, and carefully packed inside the skull, for protection.

Under Attack

Y our body has to be looked after, especially when it's under constant attack. Most of its enemies are almost invisible!

WIGGLY WORMS

Bacteria are everywhere, even inside our bodies. Some of them are good, and help us, but some of them can make us ill if they gets inside us. Not only that; you can accidently swallow tiny eggs which can grow into things like worms that can live in your intestines.

KEEP OUT

Your body has lots of ways of defending itself. Your skin is the main barrier. Also, mucus in the nose and throat traps bacteria that you breathe in. Next time you have a blocked nose, remember it's the mucus, and it's fighting on your side!

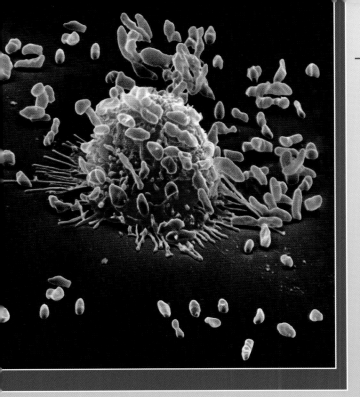

BLOOD CELLS

Despite the barriers, harmful bacteria will get into your body. Then your blood comes into play. It's made up of red and white cells. The red cells move the oxygen around the body from the lungs to where it's needed. The white cells act like security guards. They react to harmful bacteria by swallowing and destroying them.

Washing your hands is the most effective way of reducing the risk of bacterial infection.

TAKING CARE OF ME

Looking after your body isn't that difficult. Eating right, getting regular exercise and plenty of sleep will give you a better rested and fitter body. So for the sake of your own good health, hop to it!

21

Glossary

Artery
Tube forming part of the system taking blood to parts of the body

Capillary
One of the smallest of the tubes that carries blood in the body

Cartilage
Firm and flexible part of the skeleton found, for example, in the nose and ear

Membrane
Flexible lining, often containing an organ

Muscle
Band of tissue that can contract, producing movement in the body

Nutrient
Substance providing the necessary nourishment for life and growth

Organ
Part of an animal that has a specific, vital function

Receptor
Nerve ending affected by light, heat, noise and so on which it transmits to the brain by nerves

Ultraviolet
Part of the light from the Sun which can be harmful to living things

Vein
Tube forming part of the system bringing blood from parts of the body back to the heart

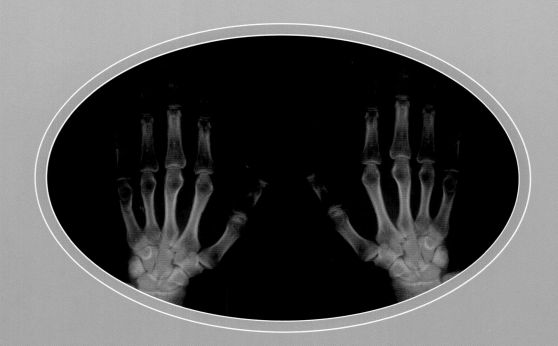

Further Reading

First Human Body Encyclopedia
Dorling Kindersley (First Reference series), 2005

The Human Body
Gallimard Jeunesse and Sylvaine Peyrois, Scholastic Reference (First Discovery series), 2007

The Usborne Complete Book of the Human Body: Internet Linked
Anna Clayborne, Stephen Moncrieff and Juliet Percival, Usborne Books, 2006

Dr Frankenstein's Human Body Book
Richard Walker and Penny Preston, Dorling Kindersley, 2008

Human Body Poster Book: Ultimate Guide to How the Body Works
John Farndon, Miles Kelly Publishing, 2006

First Encyclopedia of the Human Body
Fiona Chandler, Usborne Books (First Encyclopedias series) 2004

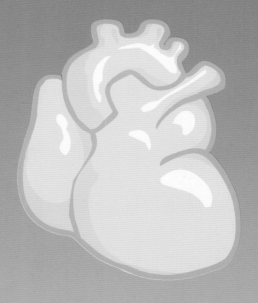

Index